CW01646586

THE SIAMESE KITTENS AND THE CHRISTMAS HEDGEHOG

Also by Michael Haykin & Chris Iliff

Reformation Lightning

The Siamese Kittens and the Breadcrumbs

The Siamese Kittens and the Snow Leopard

THE SIAMESE KITTENS AND THE CHRISTMAS HEDGEHOG

Michael A.G. Haykin

Illustrated by Chris Iliff

Reformation
Lightning

Scripture quotations have been taken from the Christian Standard Bible®, Copyright © 2017 by Holman Bible Publishers. Used by permission. Christian Standard Bible® and CSB® are federally registered trademarks of Holman Bible Publishers.

Copyright © 2023 by Michael A.G. Haykin

First published in Great Britain in 2023

The right of Michael A.G. Haykin to be identified as the Author of this Work has been asserted by him in accordance with the Copyright, Designs and Patents Act 1988.

All rights reserved. No part of this publication may be reproduced, stored in a retrieval system or transmitted in any form or by any means, electronic, mechanical, photocopying, recording or otherwise, without the prior permission of the publisher or the Copyright Licensing Agency.

British Library Cataloguing in Publication Data
A record for this book is available from the British Library

ISBN: 978-1-916669-04-8

Designed and typeset by Pete Barnsley (CreativeHoot.com)
Illustrated by Chris Iliff (ChrisIliff.co.uk)

Printed in Denmark

Reformation Lightning, an imprint of 10Publishing
Unit C, Tomlinson Road, Leyland, PR25 2DY, England

Email: info@10ofthose.com
Website: www.10ofthose.com

1 3 5 7 10 8 6 4 2

1

THE SNOW

Do you like snow? In wintertime it can be wonderful. Looking out your window you see heavy, dull grey clouds as far as your eyes can see. And then, slowly and silently, the clouds open up and it begins to snow. Flecks of white come tumbling down from those grey skies. And the brown fields, with their patches of green here and there, are soon covered with snowy blankets of white.

Mr. and Mrs. Quinn's children loved it when it snowed; it made them think of snowball fights, making snowmen, hot chocolate

by a roaring fire, and maybe even buttery toast or crumpets. As for their Siamese kittens, Siam and Ko-ko and Java, what did they think about? Well, as they watched the snow fall that first winter at the Quinns' house, their blue eyes grew wide with wonder as the world outside their house became whiter than white.

They didn't know, of course, that snow is another form of water. If they did, they might have watched with a bit of fright, for, as you know, like most cats, Siamese kittens don't like water.

But they watched that first big snowfall at the bay window overlooking the Irish Sea. They watched at the door when the Quinn kids ran outside and began to pack the snow into balls. They watched until a few flakes of the white stuff landed on Java's fine pink nose and quickly turned to water.

Aargh, he mewed, it was cold – and wet! Siam and Ko-ko laughed at Java as he jumped back from the door, mewing. He really was a scaredy-cat.

They laughed and laughed until snow began landing on them all, splattering their dark velvety paws and chocolate-coloured fur. For just a moment, the sparkling white snowflakes on their dark fur made them look like snow leopards; but then the snow was gone, and their fur was simply wet.

Ko-ko was very fussy about her fur, and when she wasn't eating or sleeping or chasing her brother or sister, she would be licking her fur, smoothing it out, removing any trace of dirt, and making herself feel nice. Now, it was okay for her to wet her fur and lick it, but to have something else making her wet, well, that was not nice at all! And she began to mew and lick and mew and lick. She really was a fussy cat.

And Siam? Well, she rolled on the ground until most of the wetness was soon gone, and she was ready for the next adventure! And what an adventure it would be. This winter, the kittens would soon discover that there are other animals who dislike being wet even more than they do…

2

THE CELLAR

Chai, if you remember, was the older Siamese cat in the large country house in which Siam and Ko-ko and Java lived. He was a very wise cat and, in the eyes of the kittens, also very old (he was actually only twelve years old in human years, but in cat years that would make him sixty-four – as old as some grandparents!).

Of course, he had seen snow before. So, instead of getting snowed on like the kittens, Chai went and stretched out in front of the big fireplace in the kitchen where Mrs. Quinn had already started a fire. On a cold wintry day, there was nothing better in Chai's mind than being warm and toasty in front of a blazing fire.

One of the things that Chai also loved doing was exploring the country house, especially

the cellar underneath, which was large and filled with boxes and interesting passageways that seemed to go on forever. Years ago, when he was a little kitten, he had discovered the joy of the cellar. Of course, it could be scary at times. What do you think Chai was scared of? Not the dark – cats have fabulous eyesight and they can see all kinds of things in the dark that we cannot. No, Chai was not afraid of the dark.

What was it, then?

Well, first of all, there were odd noises. There was an old furnace down there that sometimes

clanged

and banged.

The sound made him almost jump out of his skin if he forgot that it was only the furnace.

And then, there were the bugs...

All types of insects lived in the cellar: spiders, centipedes, flies... Chai knew enough not to eat the spiders since they could make you very sick. And Chai didn't eat the centipedes either. All those legs made his skin crawl. But the flies were yummy now and then – if he could catch them.

Occasionally, there were also mice in the cellar. But they didn't scare Chai. He would play with one if he found it, patting it back and forth between his jet-black paws and opening his mouth really wide as if he were going to eat it in one big gulp. But he never did, and after a while, he would let it go on its way.

The Quinns had hoped he would be a good mouser, but they eventually had to admit he really wasn't a good farm cat in that regard. He was too gentle to catch such timid creatures as mice.

One evening – well, it was actually Christmas Eve – Chai ventured down to the cellar to explore some of the places he had visited in the past. But no sooner had he gotten down the stairs when he smelt a smell he did not recognise. It was not a mouse; he was sure of that.

Once, many years ago, when Chai was a young, agile cat, he had met a brown rat in the cellar with a filthy pink tail. He would never forget the smell of that unpleasant meeting. But this smell was not that.

So, what was it?

3

THE STRANGER

Chai did not have to sniff around for very long. As he rounded a corner in the cellar, he saw a small, round animal with a long, funny-looking face that ended in a narrow nose, very short legs, and, most strange of all, it was covered with prickly spines. Do you know what he had met in the cellar? Of course, you do. It was a hedgehog.

But Chai had never met such a creature in all his years. It looked very odd.

"Who are you?" he blurted out.

But the hedgehog was so scared it immediately pulled in its face and rolled itself up until only its spines showed. And there it stayed, a spiky little ball.

Well, Chai, like most cats, was curious. In fact, you may have heard the saying, "Curiosity killed the cat." People started using this saying about a hundred years ago or so to warn us about the danger of looking into things that are none of our business. And that is exactly what Chai did.

After a few minutes of watching and sniffing the air, he edged closer and closer to the hedgehog. The hedgehog had not moved, for as long as he stayed rolled up with only his spines showing, he knew that he was perfectly safe.

Finally, when Chai was right next to the hedgehog, he gave it a sniff.

Boy, did he get a shock when three or four of the hedgehog's spines met his tender pink nose.

Ouch!

What kind of hairs were they, Chai thought, that sting when you touch them? Chai quickly backed away. He decided that he would wait for the hedgehog to show himself. Like most cats, Chai could be very patient when he wanted. He could wait and wait and wait – quietly and seemingly without a care in the world.

Finally, when many minutes had passed, and the hedgehog thought the coast was clear, he poked his little snout from under his spines and to his shock he saw the cat waiting there.

"As I asked before," Chai began, "who are you?"

The hedgehog was tempted to roll up into a spiky ball again, but he had second thoughts, for the cat sounded like a nice cat. And so, he decided to answer Chai and tell him the story of how he had come to be in the cellar.

4

THE HEDGEHOG'S TALE

The hedgehog's name was Quill. He had been one of six little hedgehogs born to his

mother in the springtime. Somehow, though, when he was quite young, he had gotten separated from his mother and his siblings when they had gone out foraging for food one day. So, from a very young age, he had to learn to fend for himself.

Spring turned to summer, which Quill loved, because it was warm and there were tons of things to eat: berries, fruit, mushrooms and the roots of plants, even centipedes, snails and worms. When Chai heard about Quill's diet, he began to feel a little sick.

He would never eat such things! Would you? But, as the year rolled on, summer became autumn, and the days grew shorter and colder, and eventually autumn gave way to winter. And in the winter, hedgehogs like Quill go for a long sleep that we call hibernation, which lasts for many days.

But Quill had not been long hibernating when he woke up very hungry. He was so hungry that he decided to venture out of his burrow to find a snack. He found that it was the depth of winter. The ground was frozen, so Quill was unable to find any juicy worms or wriggly centipedes. And it was snowing – the very same snow that had entranced our three Siamese kittens.

The white flakes fell so fast and quick that they soon covered Quill's tracks. The whole landscape and sky seemed to be a seamless white and Quill could no longer find his burrow. Like most hedgehogs, his eyesight was not great. And his sense of smell, which could have guided him home, had been confused by the snowfall. Quill was hopelessly lost.

The hedgehog had to spend a night in the open air, freezing and hungry, his spines covered in the powdery snow. When he awoke in the morning, he tried to find his way back to his comfy burrow. But he still had no idea where it was. All he knew was that he was desperate for warmth and sleep.

It was getting dark again when he smelt the warmth of the Quinns' house. He could not see it in the dusk of the day, but he could smell it. It smelt warm and cosy and made him miss his own family dreadfully – it had been such a long time since he had snuggled with his mother or shared jokes with his siblings. So, finding a small hole in the foundation of the cellar, he had managed to squeeze through into the warmth of the house. And it was there that Chai discovered him.

5

HOSPITALITY

Some cats can be very nasty and hiss and snarl at you. But not Chai. And not our three Siamese kittens, Siam and Ko-ko and Java. Of course, you may remember that Java sometimes liked to think he was a fierce tiger. But he was really a very loving cat.

So, when Chai heard Quill's sad tale, he felt very sorry for him. He told Quill to follow him, and together they made their way up the stairs to the kitchen.

The Quinns had placed the cats' food dishes near the kitchen's great fireplace. Our three Siamese kittens were there: Java was eating and Siam and Ko-ko were stretched out, enjoying the warmth of the fire after their adventure with the snow earlier that day. Of course, they had never seen a hedgehog and had no idea that such a strange animal existed, with hard, spiky hair! But as soon as Chai began telling them Quill's tale, they were all ears.

And when he had finished, they all looked at Quill. The hedgehog, nervous to be surrounded by such big animals, peered up at them with wide eyes.

"W-w-would I be able to sit here with you for a while?" he stuttered, partly from the cold (and partly from fear).

"We can give you more than that," Java, the ginger kitten, said. He smiled at the hedgehog and invited him closer to the hearth.

"Have some of this," Siam agreed, nudging her bowl towards him.

Overwhelmed, Quill let out a small squeak of gratitude. But the best part of all for the lost hedgehog was when the fire started to

die down and the Siamese kittens and Chai snuggled together by the glowing embers to preserve as much warmth as they could. Chai was on the verge of inviting Quill to join them, when he realized that Quill's spines would not make a good bedfellow! There was no way he wanted to be poked again by one of Quill's spines – and nor would you, I dare say. He asked the hedgehog if he could get rid of his spines, just for a bit.

"I'm afraid they don't work like that," Quill said as he shook his head.

There was a sad pause until Ko-Ko, who had a very long and fluffy tail, stuck out her tail and curled it into a spiral.

"Here," she gestured. "Try lying on this."

One by one all the cats offered their tails until Quill had a lovely soft bed on which to join the cats.

Warm and toasty, with a full and happy tummy, Quill closed his eyes. He was thankful for his new friends and their hospitality on this night we call Christmas Eve.

"I was hungry and you gave

me something to eat"

Matthew 25:35

Read more *Siamese Kittens* from Ref Light:

Reformation Lightning

Kids fiction from a biblical worldview

We create thrilling stories that point to the greatest gospel story, giving truth a clear avenue into kids' hearts and imaginations.

Reformation Lightning is an imprint of 10Publishing and its titles are available through

10ofthose.com